all about BUDVA

BUDVA CITY GUIDE

BRANKO BANJO CEJOVIC

all about BUDVA

Author: Branko BanjO Cejovic

Cover design by Olivera Cejovic
Part of text by Danilo Lekovic

Book design & Photos by Branko BanjO Cejovic
Seafood on plate photo by Petr Kratochvil

All rights reserved.

No part of this book may be reproduced in any form or by any electronic or mechanical means including information storage and retrieval systems, without permission in writing from the author. The only exception is by a reviewer, who may quote short excerpts in a review.

Published by Visit-Montenegro.com
Distributed by BritishDotCom ltd

First Digital Edition: January 2013
First Printed Edition: February 2014

ISBN-13: 978-1496127303
ISBN-10: 1496127307

Copyright © 2013 by Visit-Montenegro.com

all about BUDVA

Content

Budva	4
History	6
Legend	8
Culture	9
Nature	12
Tourism - Beaches	15
Tourism - Hotels	19
Tourism - Food and Drink	21
Tourism - Shopping	25
Tourism - Activities	27
Tourism - Top Tours	28
Tourism - Churches, Monasteries	30
Other Useful Info	32
Accommodation in Budva	33
Budva Map	55
Visit Montenegro Digital Edition	56
My Notes About Budva	57

Budva

Montenegro Coast

Budva is the metropolis of Montenegrin tourism thanks to the great number of beaches that make this a most desirable tourist destination. Apart from its natural beauty, its bay islands and beaches for example, Budva is rich in historic monuments.

The Old town lies on a small peninsula and represents a treasure chest of culture heritage. Crossed with narrow streets and squares are famous buildings, the Church Sv. Trojica, housing the tomb of the exquisite writer Stjepan Mitrov Ljubisa, the Churches of Sv. Ivan, Sv. Bogorodica and Sv. Sava. During the summer months it turns into a City Theatre with numerous local performances and

all about BUDVA

shows from abroad. In the Stari Grad (Old town) you can also visit many shops, cafés, restaurants and galleries. Monasteries Stanjevici, Podostrog, Rezevici and Gradiste are important historic and religious monuments of Budva.

The Budva coast is 21 km long with 17 beaches. It is among the most beautiful coasts in the world and its beauty will not leave you indifferent.

History

Budva – and ancient town, next to the very coast, hides a rich historical past. The distant past reaches back to the V century B.C. According to the numerous legends Budva was firstly the Illyrian town. Its first inhabitants were the King of the historically well-known Thebe – Kadmo and the Queen Harmonia.

Already in the II century B.C. Budva falls under the Romans. On its territory at that time the trading was very developed. The citizens were engaged in raising grapes and olives. After the fall of the Roman Empire, in Budva began the period of Byzantium reign. The struggle of people from Budva against Byzantium began in 535 year. The fall of the Byzantium reign happened after the arrival of the Nemanjic dynasty on the territory of the former Montenegrin coast (1184. – 1186.).

Still, the greatest bloom Budva experienced in the Middle century during the period of life of Serbian emperor Dusan. At that time Budva got its statute, in which the new conditions of life in the Middle century are described.

Under the reign of the Venetian Republic, Budva falls in 1442. Beside the oppression by the Venetians, the troubles of citizens of Budva came also from the Turks, who often invade Budva and surrounding places and they as well fight with the Venetians. Budva is bearing the brunt between the two belligerent sides, all the time until the beginning of the XVIII century.

In 1807. Budva is taken over by the French, and in 1813. it falls under the Austro – Hungarian reign, which governs Budva

all about BUDVA

for the next one hundred years. Ravaged and impoverished Budva, under the reign of the Austro – Hungary awaits the I World War, that is, the year 1914. The liberation from the Austro – Hungarian monarchy came in 1918.

Still, that was just a pause until the II World War, because already in 1941 Budva and its surrounding were again occupied, this time by Italy. The liberation from the Nazi reign Budva awaited on the 22nd of November 1944.

Legend

With the special attention Budva and people from Budva keep the mythical legend about the foundation of the town. BATH-UA, BUTOBA, BUTUA – today Budva – hides its name behind the most famous authentic story about the foundation of the town from the time of the Stefan Byzantium from the VI century.

As it s written in the incites of the Filon from Bilbos from the II century A.D., the foundation of Budva is connected to the founder of the town Thebe, a mythical personality and the son of the Phoenician King Agemor – Kadma.

Namely, Kadmo and his wife Harmonija in their old ages were exiled from Thebe and on the ox driven vehicles they directed themselves to the land of the Enheleans – the eel people, (the oldest citizens in the area of Budva), where they have founded a new town BOUTHOE – Budva.

According to the legend, it is by the oxen that Budva got its name, (Bous – in Greek Ox), which brought the spouses Kadma and Harmonija, the former rulers of Thebe, in Budva. According to some other sources, Harmojia gave birth to the son of Illyrian.

Still, because of some murder that Kadmo committed in his youth, the punishment of Gods came onto him, so the spouses (Kadmo and Harmonija), according to the legend, were turned into snakes.

all about BUDVA

Culture

Budva besides being a tourist is also a town of culture. Not only because of its extremely valuable historical past but also because of the constant influences and permeating of various cultures from the land and the sea (Helens, Venetians, French, Austro – Hungarians…), the cultural dimension of Budva has always been interwoven in the social life of the town. The authentic monuments: numerous churches, monasteries, fortresses even today testify of the past of Budva.

The most attractive and the oldest is the Old town Budva, in which the majority of those monuments are found. Beside the history and culture, the spirit of Budva was carried through the centuries by many famous personalities. Budva gave birth to numerous great man of painting brush and quill.

We shall mention some of them:

Todor Vukovic, the painter from Maine SV century, Krsto Ivanovic – the chronicler from Budva XVII century.

The far famous Conte Stjepan Zanovic lived in the XVIII century and from his early youth he was prone to challenges and adventures, unruly and dissipated life.

The important personality for Budva is also the painter who has a rich opus, Anastas Bocaric – XVII century. He got his education in Athens. He was engaged in sculpture, calligraphy and applied arts. At the same time he was the first teacher of his brother Spiro Bocaric, who got his education in Venice. He made a great number of portraits and landscapes.

Still, without any doubt, the most famous man from Budva, a literate and a diplomat, who is well known outside the borders of Montenegro, is the national tribune Stefan Mitrov Ljubisa, XIX

century.

For life that literate was proclaimed the best narrator of that era. He got famous for his notes and collections of the folk customs, events and preservation of the folk language from the oblivion.

From the more recent time, from the period of the XX century, also the recognized and famous public and scientific workers stand out. As the most significant ones we can name the brothers Miroslav and Stevan Luketic. PhD Miroslav Luketic was a famous historian, and a chronicler. His brother Stevan Luketic was a sculptor recognized in the world. Also painters Slobodan Slovnic and Jovan Ivanovic were born in Budva where they also live.

Nature

Budva is pounded by the warm Adriatic Sea. Budva Riviera encloses the surface of 122 m2.

Budva has 25 km of jagged shore. The climate in Budva is typically Mediterranean, which means that the winters are mild and the summers mostly dry and warm. Budva has 2.300 sunny hours per year.

In the sea aquatorium numerous animal and floral species live. We have green, black, and red alga. In the Budva aquatorium there are also numerous types of fishes: cipla (grey mullet (lat. Mugil cephalus)), dentex (lat. Dentex dentex), bamboo fish (lat. Sarpa salpa), granper (lat. Scorpaena scrofa), gilthead fish (lat. Sparus aurata) and even amberjack (lat. Seriola dumerili).

Often, the inhabitants of the sea bottom are also octopuses, lobsters, squids, cuttlefish, mussels, stonefishes and finger like fish.

all about BUDVA

Budva doesn't have extremely big temperature contrast, which makes it even more recommendable for tourists as an ideal place for rest. The swimming season begins on the 10th of May and lasts until the 8th of November.

Flora and fauna in Budva are similar to flora and fauna of all other coastal towns. In Budva there are palm trees, oleanders, mimosas... But also there are wild and domestic pomegranates, figs, oranges, mandarins, grapes and olive trees.

For Budva and its surrounding the raising of the very autochthonous fruit kind, which olive is, is very important. The care of olive trees lasts for centuries, and for a long time it is considered as a holy tree, as well as a tree of peace. How much it was respected in the past confirms the record that few centuries ago, especially in the Coast, a young man could not get married unless he plants 30 olive offsprings.

Along the Budva's beaches you can fell the scent of pines and cypresses. The greenery and the color, along with the scents that come

all about BUDVA

from the cypresses and pines from numerous parks in Budva, lurk numerous people who besides in swimming and the sea the enjoyment of summer vacation can experience by resting in hotel, city or forest parks. Such places are numerous, and you can find them almost in every step that you make.

Budva has also a rich fauna. In the parks you can often see squirrels, and in this area you can also see: weasel, otter, rabbit, marten, wild pig, fox even the stag with antlers, but also various kinds of birds: gulls, swallows, eagles, sparrows etc.

Tourism - Beaches

The first organized tourist arrival in Budva, are mentioned in the 1930's. The beach tourism began with the arrival of the first foreigners, Czechs, to the coast of Budva Riviera. Since then and until now Budva has largely developed, in the tourist sense. On the 12 kilometers, from Jaz to Petrovac on some 20 beaches, in the warm sun, from the 10th of May until the 8th of November you can enjoy for 182 days. Budva Riviera has the surface of 122 km2.

Budva has 25 kilometers of jagged coast. The climate in Budva is typically Mediterranean, which means that the winters are mild and summers usually dry and very hot. Budva has 2.300 sunny hours per year. The temperature of the seawater during the summer is between 21 and 25 C0.

On the Riviera with pearly beaches, as Budva is also called, we have: 2 km away from Budva is the beach Jaz, 200 meters away

all about BUDVA

from the Old town there are beaches: Mogren I and II, next to the walls of the Old town we have the beach called Ricardova glava (Richard's head). Beside the Budva Riva we have the beach Pizana, along the shore in Budva we have Slovenska plaza (Slovenian beach), and in the middle part of Budva Riviera we have Becici beach.

6 kilometers away from Budva there is the beach Kamenovo, 300 meters away we have the beach Przno, then two beaches beside the well known King's residence of Karadjordjevic – Milocer. Some 9 kilometers away from Budva there are two beaches on Sveti Stefan (St. Stefan), nudist beach Crvena glavica (Little red head), and 10 kilometers on the way from Budva to Petrovac is the beach Drobni pijesak (crushed sand).

On the other end of the municipality of Budva is Petrovac, in which we have a city beach, 500 kilometers from Petrovac we have Lucice, and 2 kilometers away is beach Buljarica.

all about BUDVA

On the greatest part of the beach there are modernly arranged (in Italian and Spanish style) beach bars. The great number of beaches has blue flags, which is a guarantee of their high quality

all about BUDVA

and great comfort. On all the mentioned beaches there are lifeguards who are observing the swimmers and are taking care of them.

For others, who like more peaceful places, the drives and swimming on the Island Sveti Nikola (St. Nikola), popularly called Hawaii are offered, as well as the boat or barge driving along the Montenegrin coast. If you are a lover of intimate places, along the Budva Riviera there are numerous hidden coves, and maybe some still undiscovered places for swimming and resting, as well as the beaches that are maybe just waiting for you. The number of beaches, on which mostly young people go, is also big. On those beaches you feel as if you are on the most exotic world places. Techno, rave, hip – hop parties that are meant to last during the night often are prolonged, so they last even during the day. For a good atmosphere on the beaches DJ's are in charge. The loud music is characteristic for cafés and mini – bars, but also for the opened terraces along the Budva promenade, and he promenade towards the Old town and Becici.

Tourism - Hotels

For the accommodation of guests Budva offers almost everything, from the accommodation in the hotels that have 5 or 4 stars, for the tourists with the refined demands, to the accommodation in the private rooms, villas and apartments, in which you can spend your summer vacation at some very favorable prices.

In the narrow and wider center of Budva there are great number of hotels. According to the last data there are about 60 hotels. The majority of hotels, more precisely 16 of them have 3 stars. There are 11 hotels that have 4 stars.

Hotel rooms and apartments will attract your attention already during your first encounter with them. The majority of the hotels has their own parking lot, rent – a – car services, their own beach, saunas, opened and indoor pools, terrains for mini sports, halls for recreation, open terraces etc…

According to the opinion of the tourist commission for standardization of 19 hotel facilities, in Budva only two of them got two stars while 7 of them in Budva and the surrounding got one star. In the mentioned facilities you can rest and spend your vacation ate extremely favorable prices.

Except in the hotels at somewhat favorable prices you can spend your summer vacation in private accommodation. The exact number of house facilities that are being rented is changing every year, and their exact number still cannot be completely determined. According to the records of the Budva's Association of tourist agencies, in Budva and the surrounding there are between 100 and 120.000 beds that are meant for renting.

List of 10 best hotels in Budva:

- Hotel Astoria,
- Sentido Tara Hotel,
- The Queen of Montenegro,
- Hotel Slovenska Plaza LUX,
- Sveti Stefan,
- Maestral,
- Iberostar Bellevue,
- Splendid Conference & Spa,
- Avala Resort & Villas,
- Hotel Montenegro.

Tourism – Food and Drink

In almost all tourist restaurant facilities along the Budva Riviera, at any time day or night you can enjoy in numerous domestic cuisine specialties.

If you are a guest that is for the first time visiting Montenegro or Budva, the heads of the house will welcome you with fritters (sweet small round sweet) and homemade honey with the domestic brandy, made of the first class grape, often on the table you will find dried figs, that were picked in the previous summer, dried on the sun and in the wind, of very sweet taste and alluring scent.

all about BUDVA

If your visit to Budva is longer than just a passing by, we are sure that you won't go back to the country from which you are coming without trying the domestic smoked ham (dried pork meat) or domestic goat or cow cheese, and special cheese that is kept in the olive oil. The mentioned supplies are both tasty food and a pleasure for your eyes, especially when all those scents and tastes are found in one place, nicely served with some leaf of green salad, parsley, green and black olives, surrounded by the bottles and glasses of the original red vine like: "Krtsac", "Procorden", or white vine "Krstac".

all about BUDVA

Already after a several days of your staying, you must not forget the fact that you are on the Mediterranean, and that the cuisine in Budva is traditionally and mostly coastal. As the sea aquatorium is rich with fish, unavoidably you have to try at least some of the sea fruits like for e.g. octopus salad, black rice, mussels in a sauce, dentex, or some other fish on the grill. Scented branches of the

all about BUDVA

rosemary, chopped parsley, garlic, lime, and great amounts of olive oil are the basic ingredients for the just caught fish to be tastefully prepared.

The choice of the restaurants, hotels or other facilities in which you will enjoy trying the sea fruits we leave to you.

Still, it is up to us to briefly remind you that the fish is swimming three times: first in the sea, then in the oil, and just then it swims in vine. With various kinds of fishes various vines are suitable, but we will leave that to the skillful gastronome in Budva Riviera. Whatever drink you choose, you will traditionally have to give a toast to yourself and the others, for good health, luck, advancement in work, and maybe even for the new encounter with Budva Riviera, who knows…

Tourism - Shopping

The largest part of the shops and boutiques that offer the wide spectrum of the choice of the wardrobe mostly of all the world fashion designers and creators, of all patterns, colors and styles, can be found in Budva's Old town. Nicely arranged boutiques and store windows are alike to numerous shops in world metropolises. Next to those shops there are perfume shops, which offer the products of the distinguished cosmetic brands, jewelry shops, photograph shops, bookshops, libraries, children boutiques, cafés, pizzerias etc...

If you get tired of going through boutiques in the Old Budva's town, or down the main promenade that is next to the shore, you can also shop on the summer bazaar.

The summer bazaar is situated next to the Budva's prom-

enade, and it offers various goods, clothes, gallantry, beach equipment, various souvenirs etc…

Not far from the Old town there are also several selling objects, and a city market.

Finally, in Budva, you can enjoy in small shopping center: TQ PLAZA near main Post Office. This nice and pleasant place offer wide range of nice shops and nice cafes and restaurants.

Tourism – Activities

If your characteristics are strong will, persistency, courage, extra energy and the desire for the adrenaline, Budva is surely the place for you. Probably the words like: paragliding, aqua ski, bungee jumping... sound interesting to you, but if you experience all of that in one day, on one place, then that is the reason for you to com e to Budva and feel the allures of those challenges.

The ride with the paraglide begins at 760 meters above sea level from the take over point on Brajici. Stirring the paraglide with the aid of the instructor, you will have a chance to enjoy in the unforgettable and alluring sights on Budva Riviera.

The excitement will be if you decide for bungee – jumping. The platform which is 40 meters high, and is situated not far away from the cove in the ending part of the Slovenska beach.

Budva is ready for the water skiers. Aqua ski cable railway is situated on the Becici beach. The cable railway offers possibilities of great fun to all of those who wish to have an active and more exciting vacation in Budva Riviera. Aqua ski cable railway is meant for the curious tourists as well as to the top sportsmen, and beginners, because the trainee instructors are always on the spot, present.

For the lovers of depths in Budva there are several diving clubs. With the professional and expert aid they offer the entire training and adequate equipment. As the water temperature during the summer goes from 21 to 25C the diving is more than pleasing and it simply attracts you to research the depths.

Tourism – Top Tours

For the guests who wish to research and recreate themselves in their own choice, Budva offers also a very simple way of recreation in nature. By walking from the Old Budva's town over the Slovenska plaza (Slovenian beach), by climbing up the hill Zavala, you can reach Becici and Rafailovici.

If you do not wish to set yourself in that direction on foot, you won't feel less joy if you go to visit that part of Budva by a tourist mini train.

If you have a wish to meet the history of some other part of Montenegro besides the history of Budva, numerous tourist agencies offer various arrangements, and often, the individuals, along the Slovenian coast, make those arrangements. Those arrangements offer rafting down the River Tara, visits to the museums, monasteries, drives along the Skadar Lake…

But if you wish to meet Budva, especially its hidden places, like rocky coves, the real solution is the touring of Budva Riviera by some of the numerous tourist taxi boats. Such an arrangement includes the visit of one of the numerous Budva's beaches like beach Jaz. Beach in Becici, Sveti Stefan beach, Drobni pijesak, or Petrovac.

If you wish to have an easy ride for two and if you wish to enjoy on the Island Sveti Nikola for e.g. take advantage of the possibility of renting some of the numerous taxi barges, whose drivers are ready to take you to a certain destination, beach, or cape at almost any time day or night, for you to swim in depths, or to cruise over the sea.

Also, beside the Budva, in the same way you can get acquainted with the Bar or Herceg Novi Riviera. Numerous trip boats which can take 25 - 30 passengers, offer a high quality trips to Herceg Novi or Bar with the staying of an hour in the mentioned towns.

If you wish to create your day in some other way or you simply want to reach a certain beach, or cape in a different way the simplest way to do that is to use the ride of taxi – vans, which drive on the relation Budva – Becici, or Budva – Sveti Stefan, or Budva – Petrovac, in every 15 minutes or maybe half an hour.

Also for the ride to the desired hotel, restaurant, or privately rented apartment, you can go by numerous taxis that are found only couple of hundreds of meters away from the Old town of Budva.

all about BUDVA

Tourism - Churches, Monasteries

About the tumultuous history of Budva and its surrounding, today numerous cultural monuments testify. Budva has a great number of culturally – historical monuments, among which a great number of them are monasteries and smaller churches. All those monuments lively document the past historical and social happenings in the area of Budva Riviera. Among the most famous culturally historical monuments we can count in: the Church of Sveti Jovan (St. Jovan), which was built on the VII century, the Church Santa Maria from Punta dating from 840. Year A.D., and the Church of Sveto Trojstvo (St. Trinity) dating from 1804.

North from Budva there is monastery Stanjevici. In which the first Montenegrin Legal code was voted in 1798. The most important and the most frequently mentioned monastery, the literacy center of Pastrovici, the tribe which for a long time had the autono-

all about BUDVA

mous municipality made of 12 villages, and which fought against all the conquerors: the Turks, the Venetians, the pirates, later the Austrians, and the Italians, is found above the town – hotel Sveti Stefan. It is made of three churches in which there are some frescoes dating from the XVII century.

Very luxurious is also monastery Rezevici between Sveti Stefan and Petrovac, whose architecture reaches back to the XIII century. Not far from Petrovac is monastery Gradiste, a monument of the late Middle Century.

Still, the great number of churches and monasteries which are found all over Budva Riviera, and that are waiting for all those tourists to whom sightseeing of the culturally historical monuments is much more than just a pleasure.

Other Useful Info

As we say, Budva is one of top tourist places in Montenegro, especially for young people who like active holiday with lot of entreatments, open discotheques, modern cafes, many beach activities etc.

Budva offer great holiday and from Budva you can visit also many attractive places in Montenegro by organized tours.

Accommodation in Budva

Budva offer wide range of accommodation. We suggest you to make ONLINE BOOKING because this is best way to get great price and to get good accommodation. Online Booking service do not offer only expensive hotels. You can find lot of small private apartments with great service and affordable prices.

We present you list of all available hotels in Budva (from March 2013) with appropriate links to online booking web pages:

Abeona Apartments   http://www.booking.com/hotel/me/abeona-apartmani.html?aid=323220

Accommodation Kruna   http://www.booking.com/hotel/me/gostionica-kruna-becici.html?aid=323220

Adelisa Apartments   http://www.booking.com/hotel/me/adelisa-apartments.html?aid=323220

Ajko Panorama Apartments   http://www.booking.com/hotel/me/panorama-budva.html?aid=323220

Alexandar Montenegro Luxury Suites & Spa   http://www.booking.com/hotel/me/alexandarsuits.html?aid=323220

Apartmani Mirenza   http://www.booking.com/hotel/me/mirenza.html?aid=323220

Apartmani Miron   http://www.booking.com/hotel/me/miron.html?aid=323220

Apartmani Plima   http://www.booking.com/hotel/

me/apartmani-plima.html?aid=323220

Apartmani Djuric http://www.booking.com/hotel/me/apartmani-auria.html?aid=323220

Apartment Adriatic Residence http://www.booking.com/hotel/me/2-bdrs-apartment-budva.html?aid=323220

Apartment Budva Rafailovici http://www.booking.com/hotel/me/apartment-budva-rafailovici.html?aid=323220

Apartment Marko http://www.booking.com/hotel/me/apartmani-budva-budva4.html?aid=323220

Apartment Mega http://www.booking.com/hotel/me/apartman-mega.html?aid=323220

Apartment Rozino Marko http://www.booking.com/hotel/me/rozino-marko.html?aid=323220

Apartments A&S Montenegro http://www.booking.com/hotel/me/apartments-a-amp-s-montenegro.html?aid=323220

Apartments Aleksic Old Town http://www.booking.com/hotel/me/lux-apartmani.html?aid=323220

Apartments Alexandra http://www.booking.com/hotel/me/apartmenthouse-alexandra.html?aid=323220

Apartments and Rooms Vujacic http://www.booking.com/hotel/me/vila-vujacic.html?aid=323220

Apartments Andrija http://www.booking.com/hotel/me/kuaa-beaiai.html?aid=323220

Apartments Angela http://www.booking.com/hotel/

me/apartments-angela.html?aid=323220

Apartments Angelina   http://www.booking.com/hotel/me/apartmani-angelina.html?aid=323220

Apartments Anita   http://www.booking.com/hotel/me/apartmani-anita-budva.html?aid=323220

Apartments Andjela   http://www.booking.com/hotel/me/apartmani-andjela.html?aid=323220

Apartments Azzuro   http://www.booking.com/hotel/me/apartmani-azzuro.html?aid=323220

Apartments Becic   http://www.booking.com/hotel/me/apartmani-beaia.html?aid=323220

Apartments Bella   http://www.booking.com/hotel/me/apartments-bella.html?aid=323220

Apartments Bjelanovichttp://www.booking.com/hotel/me/apartmanibjelanovic.html?aid=323220

Apartments Bonus   http://www.booking.com/hotel/me/bonus.html?aid=323220

Apartments Boreta   http://www.booking.com/hotel/me/apartmani-boreta-krsto.html?aid=323220

Apartments Boreta II   http://www.booking.com/hotel/me/apartmani-boreta-ii.html?aid=323220

Apartments Boss   http://www.booking.com/hotel/me/apartmani-boss.html?aid=323220

Apartments Bocovic   http://www.booking.com/hotel/

me/apartmani-boa3-4ovia.html?aid=323220

Apartments Branko   http://www.booking.com/hotel/me/smjea-taj-ana.html?aid=323220

Apartments Bu2   http://www.booking.com/hotel/me/apartmani-budva-budva.html?aid=323220

Apartments Budva Center   http://www.booking.com/hotel/me/apartmani-budva-centar.html?aid=323220

Apartments Budva Center 2   http://www.booking.com/hotel/me/apartments-budva-centre-2.html?aid=323220

Apartments Budva Na Dlanu http://www.booking.com/hotel/me/budva-na-dlan.html?aid=323220

Apartments Butua   http://www.booking.com/hotel/me/butua.html?aid=323220

Apartments Casa Natale   http://www.booking.com/hotel/me/casa-natale.html?aid=323220

Apartments Cenic   http://www.booking.com/hotel/me/apartments-cenic.html?aid=323220

Apartments City   http://www.booking.com/hotel/me/apartments-sity-2.html?aid=323220

Apartments Crystall   http://www.booking.com/hotel/me/apartmani-crystall.html?aid=323220

Apartments Decic   http://www.booking.com/hotel/me/apartmani-decic.html?aid=323220

Apartments Djedovic http://www.booking.com/hotel/

me/apartmani-budva-budva3.html?aid=323220

Apartments Elena http://www.booking.com/hotel/me/villa-elena-budva.html?aid=323220

Apartments Family http://www.booking.com/hotel/me/apartmani-family.html?aid=323220

Apartments Fjondra http://www.booking.com/hotel/me/apartmani-beaia-budva.html?aid=323220

Apartments Gold http://www.booking.com/hotel/me/vila-bagi.html?aid=323220

Apartments Grgurovichttp://www.booking.com/hotel/me/apartmani-grgurovic.html?aid=323220

Apartments HMD http://www.booking.com/hotel/me/apartments-hdm-budva.html?aid=323220

Apartments Holiday http://www.booking.com/hotel/me/apartmani-vua-urovia.html?aid=323220

Apartments Inspiration http://www.booking.com/hotel/me/inspiration.html?aid=323220

Apartments Iric http://www.booking.com/hotel/me/apartmani-iric.html?aid=323220

Apartments Ivan http://www.booking.com/hotel/me/apartmani-ivan.html?aid=323220

Apartments Ivanovic http://www.booking.com/hotel/me/villa-ivanovic-12.html?aid=323220

Apartments Jelena http://www.booking.com/hotel/

me/apartmani-jelena.html?aid=323220

Apartments Kalluka   http://www.booking.com/hotel/me/kalluka.html?aid=323220

Apartments Kamena Njiva   http://www.booking.com/hotel/me/dd-d-d-ddeg-kamena-njiva.html?aid=323220

Apartments Knezevic http://www.booking.com/hotel/me/apartments-knezevic.html?aid=323220

Apartments Krapina   http://www.booking.com/hotel/me/vila-krapina.html?aid=323220

Apartments Kucice Boljacin Do   http://www.booking.com/hotel/me/kuaice-boljaain-do.html?aid=323220

Apartments Kuljaca   http://www.booking.com/hotel/me/apartmani-kuljaca.html?aid=323220

Apartments Kunjic   http://www.booking.com/hotel/me/apartmani-kunjic.html?aid=323220

Apartments Lazar   http://www.booking.com/hotel/me/lazar-apartmani.html?aid=323220

Apartments Leonora   http://www.booking.com/hotel/me/leonora.html?aid=323220

Apartments Lungo Mare   http://www.booking.com/hotel/me/lungo-mare.html?aid=323220

Apartments Mara   http://www.booking.com/hotel/me/villa-mara.html?aid=323220

Apartments Maric   http://www.booking.com/hotel/

me/apartman-maric.html?aid=323220

Apartments Marija	http://www.booking.com/hotel/me/villa-marija.html?aid=323220

Apartments Marija	http://www.booking.com/hotel/me/marija-budva.html?aid=323220

Apartments Marina	http://www.booking.com/hotel/me/apartments-marina-budva.html?aid=323220

Apartments Markicevic	http://www.booking.com/hotel/me/apartmani-markiaevia.html?aid=323220

Apartments Markovic	http://www.booking.com/hotel/me/apartmani-markovia.html?aid=323220

Apartments Maša	http://www.booking.com/hotel/me/maa-a-apartmani.html?aid=323220

Apartments Memic	http://www.booking.com/hotel/me/memic-apartments.html?aid=323220

Apartments Memidz	http://www.booking.com/hotel/me/apartmani-memida3-4.html?aid=323220

Apartments Mikovic	http://www.booking.com/hotel/me/vila-mikovia.html?aid=323220

Apartments Mila	http://www.booking.com/hotel/me/apartmani-kotor-krimovice-bb.html?aid=323220

Apartments MM	http://www.booking.com/hotel/me/mm-apartments.html?aid=323220

Apartments Nikcevic	http://www.booking.com/hotel/

me/apartmani-nikcevic-becici-budva.html?aid=323220

Apartments Nikvik http://www.booking.com/hotel/me/nikvik.html?aid=323220

Apartments Paradiso http://www.booking.com/hotel/me/anci.html?aid=323220

Apartments Pejovic http://www.booking.com/hotel/me/apartments-pejovic.html?aid=323220

Apartments Pekovic http://www.booking.com/hotel/me/nada-pekovic.html?aid=323220

Apartments Popovic http://www.booking.com/hotel/me/apartmani-popovia-budva.html?aid=323220

Apartments Radevic http://www.booking.com/hotel/me/apartments-radevic.html?aid=323220

Apartments Radulovic http://www.booking.com/hotel/me/apartmani-radulovia.html?aid=323220

Apartments Rafailovici Central http://www.booking.com/hotel/me/rafailovici-central.html?aid=323220

Apartments Raicevic http://www.booking.com/hotel/me/apartmani-raiaevia.html?aid=323220

Apartments Savina http://www.booking.com/hotel/me/apartment-savina.html?aid=323220

Apartments Simic http://www.booking.com/hotel/me/simia3-4.html?aid=323220

Apartments Sofija http://www.booking.com/hotel/

me/apartmani-sofija.html?aid=323220

Apartments Stanivukovic http://www.booking.com/hotel/me/apartments-stanivukovic.html?aid=323220

Apartments Stanka http://www.booking.com/hotel/me/stanka.html?aid=323220

Apartments Stefan http://www.booking.com/hotel/me/stefan.html?aid=323220

Apartments Stevic - Monaco http://www.booking.com/hotel/me/apartments-stevia-monaco.html?aid=323220

Apartments Sun Seoce http://www.booking.com/hotel/me/sunseoce.html?aid=323220

Apartments Svorcan http://www.booking.com/hotel/me/apartments-svorcan.html?aid=323220

Apartments Teona http://www.booking.com/hotel/me/vila-teona.html?aid=323220

Apartments Three Star http://www.booking.com/hotel/me/apartments-three-star.html?aid=323220

Apartments Tipon http://www.booking.com/hotel/me/apartment-tipon.html?aid=323220

Apartments TMV Dragovic http://www.booking.com/hotel/me/apartmani-dragovic-budva.html?aid=323220

Apartments Veronica http://www.booking.com/hotel/me/apartmani-veronika.html?aid=323220

Apartments Vidikovac http://www.booking.com/hotel/

me/apartments-vidikovac.html?aid=323220

Apartments Villa Andjela   http://www.booking.com/hotel/me/apartments-vila-andjela.html?aid=323220

Apartments Villa Blazic   http://www.booking.com/hotel/me/villa-blazic.html?aid=323220

Apartments Villa Elmira   http://www.booking.com/hotel/me/villa-elmira.html?aid=323220

Apartments Villa M Palace   http://www.booking.com/hotel/me/villa-m-palace.html?aid=323220

Apartments Vjera   http://www.booking.com/hotel/me/vjera.html?aid=323220

Apartments Zorana   http://www.booking.com/hotel/me/apartmani-zorana.html?aid=323220

Apia Residence   http://www.booking.com/hotel/me/villa-apia.html?aid=323220

Avala Resort & Villas   http://www.booking.com/hotel/me/avala-resort-villas.html?aid=323220

Azzuro Lux Apartments   http://www.booking.com/hotel/me/azzuro-lux-apartments.html?aid=323220

B&B Apart Hotel Paštrovski Konak   http://www.booking.com/hotel/me/pastrovski-konak.html?aid=323220

Belvedere Apartments http://www.booking.com/hotel/me/belvedere.html?aid=323220

Bjelica Apartment   http://www.booking.com/hotel/

me/bjelica-apartments.html?aid=323220

Bliss Apartments http://www.booking.com/hotel/me/bliss-apartmani.html?aid=323220

Bravo Apartments http://www.booking.com/hotel/me/vila-bravo-budva.html?aid=323220

Butua Residence http://www.booking.com/hotel/me/butua-residence.html?aid=323220

Captain Apartments http://www.booking.com/hotel/me/captain-apartments.html?aid=323220

Contessa Apartments http://www.booking.com/hotel/me/contessa-apartmani.html?aid=323220

D&D Apartments Budva http://www.booking.com/hotel/me/d-d-apartments.html?aid=323220

D&M Apartments http://www.booking.com/hotel/me/d-amp-s-amartmani.html?aid=323220

D&R Boreta Apartments http://www.booking.com/hotel/me/d-amp-r-boreta.html?aid=323220

Dimic Ellite Accommodation http://www.booking.com/hotel/me/dimia-ellite.html?aid=323220

El Mar Apartments http://www.booking.com/hotel/me/apartments-sudjic.html?aid=323220

Etno Village Pobori http://www.booking.com/hotel/me/etno-selo-pobori-budva.html?aid=323220

Franeta Apartments http://www.booking.com/hotel/

me/franeta-apartments.html?aid=323220

Garni Hotel Mena	http://www.booking.com/hotel/me/mena.html?aid=323220

Giardino Apartments	http://www.booking.com/hotel/me/giardino-apartmani.html?aid=323220

Giovani Apartments	http://www.booking.com/hotel/me/giovani.html?aid=323220

Guest House Asovic	http://www.booking.com/hotel/me/kuca-budva1.html?aid=323220

Guest House Budva Montenegro	http://www.booking.com/hotel/me/housebudva-montenegro.html?aid=323220

Guest House Ckuljevic	http://www.booking.com/hotel/me/vila-ckuljevic.html?aid=323220

Guest House Mudreša	http://www.booking.com/hotel/me/a1-2ivana-mudrea-a.html?aid=323220

Guest House Vojinovic	http://www.booking.com/hotel/me/apartmani-vojinovia.html?aid=323220

Guest House Win	http://www.booking.com/hotel/me/apartmani-win.html?aid=323220

Guesthouse Adrovic	http://www.booking.com/hotel/me/vila-adrovic.html?aid=323220

Guesthouse BMB Bagaric	http://www.booking.com/hotel/me/bmb-bagaric.html?aid=323220

Guesthouse Kuljace 2	http://www.booking.com/hotel/

me/apartmani-kuljace-2.html?aid=323220

Guesthouse Olga http://www.booking.com/hotel/me/garni-olga.html?aid=323220

Guesthouse Orlovic http://www.booking.com/hotel/me/vila-orlovia.html?aid=323220

Guesthouse Stancic http://www.booking.com/hotel/me/stancic.html?aid=323220

Hotel Admiral http://www.booking.com/hotel/me/admiral-montenegro.html?aid=323220

Hotel Aleksandar http://www.booking.com/hotel/me/aleksandar.html?aid=323220

Hotel Anita http://www.booking.com/hotel/me/anita.html?aid=323220

Hotel Aruba http://www.booking.com/hotel/me/aruba.html?aid=323220

Hotel Astoria http://www.booking.com/hotel/me/astoria.html?aid=323220

Hotel BIP http://www.booking.com/hotel/me/bip-budva.html?aid=323220

Hotel Blue Star http://www.booking.com/hotel/me/blue-star.html?aid=323220

Hotel Dubrava http://www.booking.com/hotel/me/dubrava.html?aid=323220

Hotel Garni Fineso http://www.booking.com/hotel/

me/garni-fineso.html?aid=323220

Hotel Grbalj   http://www.booking.com/hotel/me/grbalj.html?aid=323220

Hotel Kangaroo   http://www.booking.com/hotel/me/kangaroo.html?aid=323220

Hotel Kuc   http://www.booking.com/hotel/me/m-kuc.html?aid=323220

Hotel La Porta   http://www.booking.com/hotel/me/la-porta.html?aid=323220

Hotel Loza   http://www.booking.com/hotel/me/loza.html?aid=323220

Hotel Lucic   http://www.booking.com/hotel/me/l-ucic.html?aid=323220

Hotel Magnolija   http://www.booking.com/hotel/me/magnolija.html?aid=323220

Hotel Max Prestige   http://www.booking.com/hotel/me/max-prestige.html?aid=323220

Hotel Montenegro   http://www.booking.com/hotel/me/montenegro.html?aid=323220

Hotel Nion   http://www.booking.com/hotel/me/nion.html?aid=323220

Hotel Oaza   http://www.booking.com/hotel/me/oaza.html?aid=323220

Hotel Obala   http://www.booking.com/hotel/me/obala.html?aid=323220

Hotel Oliva	http://www.booking.com/hotel/me/oliva.html?aid=323220

Hotel Podostrog	http://www.booking.com/hotel/me/podostrog.html?aid=323220

Hotel Princ	http://www.booking.com/hotel/me/princ.html?aid=323220

Hotel Regina Elena	http://www.booking.com/hotel/me/regina-elena.html?aid=323220

Hotel Šajo	http://www.booking.com/hotel/me/sajo.html?aid=323220

Hotel Slovenska Plaza http://www.booking.com/hotel/me/slovenska-plaza.html?aid=323220

Hotel Slovenska Plaza Lux	http://www.booking.com/hotel/me/slovenska-plaza-lux.html?aid=323220

Hotel Stella di Mare	http://www.booking.com/hotel/me/stella-di-mare.html?aid=323220

Hotel Tatjana	http://www.booking.com/hotel/me/tatjana.html?aid=323220

Hotel Vila Lux	http://www.booking.com/hotel/me/vila-lux-budva.html?aid=323220

Iberostar Bellevue	http://www.booking.com/hotel/me/bellevue.html?aid=323220

Irish Apartment	http://www.booking.com/hotel/

me/irish-appartments.html?aid=323220

Jaz Apartments http://www.booking.com/hotel/me/jaz-apartments.html?aid=323220

Kika Rooms http://www.booking.com/hotel/me/kika.html?aid=323220

Lero Apartments http://www.booking.com/hotel/me/art-house-budva.html?aid=323220

Lighthouse Apartments http://www.booking.com/hotel/me/lighthouse.html?aid=323220

London Apartment http://www.booking.com/hotel/me/london-apartment.html?aid=323220

Lyon Apartments http://www.booking.com/hotel/me/lyon-apartmani.html?aid=323220

M-Club Rooms http://www.booking.com/hotel/me/sobe-m-club-plaza-jaz-budva.html?aid=323220

Marinero Apartments http://www.booking.com/hotel/me/marinero-apartments.html?aid=323220

Martinovic Rooms http://www.booking.com/hotel/me/villa-martinovia.html?aid=323220

Mediteran Conference & Spa Resort and Aqua Park http://www.booking.com/hotel/me/mediteran.html?aid=323220

Meridian Hotel http://www.booking.com/hotel/me/meridian.html?aid=323220

Mijovic Apartments http://www.booking.com/hotel/

me/mijovic-aparments.html?aid=323220

Mila & Jovana Apartments   http://www.booking.com/hotel/me/mila-i-jovana.html?aid=323220

Mojo Budva   http://www.booking.com/hotel/me/mojo-budva.html?aid=323220

Montenegro Hostel Budva   http://www.booking.com/hotel/me/montenegro-hostel-budva.html?aid=323220

Monterus Apartments http://www.booking.com/hotel/me/monterus.html?aid=323220

Montesa Apartments   http://www.booking.com/hotel/me/montesa-apartmani.html?aid=323220

Nikolay Boreti Apartments   http://www.booking.com/hotel/me/nikolay-boreti-budva.html?aid=323220

Panorama Apartments http://www.booking.com/hotel/me/panorama-appartments.html?aid=323220

Podmaine Suites   http://www.booking.com/hotel/me/podmaine-suites.html?aid=323220

R-Club Old Town Apartments   http://www.booking.com/hotel/me/r-club-apartmani.html?aid=323220

Radonjic Apartments   http://www.booking.com/hotel/me/radonjic-apartments.html?aid=323220

Residence Celebic-Radovic   http://www.booking.com/hotel/me/vila-celebic-radovic.html?aid=323220

Rooms and Apartments Oregon   h t t p : / / w w w .

booking.com/hotel/me/rooms-and-apartments-oregon.html?aid=323220

Rooms Casper 1	http://www.booking.com/hotel/me/casper-1.html?aid=323220

Rooms Casper 3	http://www.booking.com/hotel/me/casper-3.html?aid=323220

Rooms Domador Becici	http://www.booking.com/hotel/me/domador.html?aid=323220

Rooms Ivanovic	http://www.booking.com/hotel/me/vila-ivanovic.html?aid=323220

Rooms Limina http://www.booking.com/hotel/me/limina-rafailovici.html?aid=323220

Rooms Stefa & Ilija	http://www.booking.com/hotel/me/rooms-stefa-ilija.html?aid=323220

Rossa Apartments	http://www.booking.com/hotel/me/sofija-apartmani.html?aid=323220

Saki Apartments Budva	http://www.booking.com/hotel/me/saki-apartmani.html?aid=323220

Sea-N-Sun Apartments	http://www.booking.com/hotel/me/sea-n-sun-apartments.html?aid=323220

Sentido Tara Hotel	http://www.booking.com/hotel/me/tara.html?aid=323220

Sky View Luxury Apartments	http://www.booking.com/hotel/me/sky-view-luxury-apartments.html?aid=323220

Spa Resort Becici   http://www.booking.com/hotel/me/spa-resort-becici.html?aid=323220

Splendid Conference & Spa Resort   http://www.booking.com/hotel/me/splendid-confetence-spa-resort.html?aid=323220

Springs Apartments   http://www.booking.com/hotel/me/springs-apartments.html?aid=323220

Stella Marina Apartments   http://www.booking.com/hotel/me/stella-marina.html?aid=323220

Studio Irina   http://www.booking.com/hotel/me/apartments-irina.html?aid=323220

Studios Klementina Nikvalentin   http://www.booking.com/hotel/me/apartmani-klementina-nikvalentin.html?aid=323220

Sun Hostel Budva   http://www.booking.com/hotel/me/sun-hostel-budva.html?aid=323220

The Franeta Apartments Lux   http://www.booking.com/hotel/me/the-franeta-s-apartments-lux.html?aid=323220

The Littlest Hobo   http://www.booking.com/hotel/me/the-littlest-hobo.html?aid=323220

The Old Town Terrace Apartments   http://www.booking.com/hotel/me/the-old-town-terrace.html?aid=323220

The Queen Of Montenegro   http://www.booking.com/hotel/me/the-queen-of-montenegro.html?aid=323220

Top Jaz Apartments http://www.booking.com/hotel/me/top-jaz-apartments.html?aid=323220

Victoria Apartments http://www.booking.com/hotel/me/victoria-apartments.html?aid=323220

Vidikovac Suites http://www.booking.com/hotel/me/vidikovac-suites.html?aid=323220

Vila Galileo http://www.booking.com/hotel/me/vila-galileo.html?aid=323220

Vila Medenica http://www.booking.com/hotel/me/vila-medenica.html?aid=323220

Vila Milna 1 http://www.booking.com/hotel/me/milna-apartments.html?aid=323220

Vila Milna 2 http://www.booking.com/hotel/me/vila-milna-2.html?aid=323220

Vila Simona Lux http://www.booking.com/hotel/me/vila-simona.html?aid=323220

Villa Arigant http://www.booking.com/hotel/me/vila-arigant.html?aid=323220

Villa Bojana http://www.booking.com/hotel/me/villa-bojana.html?aid=323220

Villa Budvanka http://www.booking.com/hotel/me/villa-budvanka.html?aid=323220

Villa Castel Lapcici http://www.booking.com/hotel/me/castel-lapaiai.html?aid=323220

Villa Cucuk http://www.booking.com/hotel/me/vila-cucuk.html?aid=323220

Villa Gaga http://www.booking.com/hotel/me/villa-gaga.html?aid=323220

Villa Gaga 2 http://www.booking.com/hotel/me/villa-gaga-2.html?aid=323220

Villa Ksenija http://www.booking.com/hotel/me/villa-ksenija.html?aid=323220

Villa Markovic http://www.booking.com/hotel/me/markovic.html?aid=323220

Villa Perla Di Mare http://www.booking.com/hotel/me/villa-perla-di-mare.html?aid=323220

Villa Petranovic http://www.booking.com/hotel/me/vila-petranovic.html?aid=323220

Villa San Marco http://www.booking.com/hotel/me/villa-san-marco.html?aid=323220

Villa Seka http://www.booking.com/hotel/me/apartmani-budva.html?aid=323220

Villa Spas http://www.booking.com/hotel/me/villa-spas.html?aid=323220

Villa Sveti Nikola http://www.booking.com/hotel/me/villa-sveti-nikola.html?aid=323220

Villa Varajic Studios http://www.booking.com/hotel/me/vila-varajic.html?aid=323220

Zenovic House http://www.booking.com/hotel/me/zenovia-house.html?aid=323220

Zodiac Apartments http://www.booking.com/hotel/me/zodiac.html?aid=323220

Djakovic Apartments http://www.booking.com/hotel/me/aakovia-apartments.html?aid=323220

We also recommend you to check best online booking service on for updated information about all available hotels in Budva and other destination: **http://www.visit-montenegro.com**

Also, if you want to use rental car service, we recommend : **http://www.visit-montenegro.com**

If you have some specific demands, we recommend to contact: **http://www.visit-montenegro.com**

Budva Map

Because of specific type of ebooks, we can not provide quality and high res Map of Budva, but in this printed edition, we present you nice useful map od Budva Old Town.

Also we give you couple of links where you can find excellent city maps of Budva.

LINK 1: Google Budva Map

City map provided by Google Map Service is best for make complete impression of Budva city: **https://maps.google.com**

LINK 2: Accommodation Budva Map

This is great interactive map with all available accommodation in Budva. With one click you can get all information about every hotel, motel, apartment, see prices and make online booking. This map you can find on: **http://www.Visit-Montenegro.com**

LINK 3: Online Shop with Paper Maps

In this online shop, you can find and order many paper materials from Montenegro, like maps, guides, books, postcards, souvenirs, etc : **http://Shop.Visit-Montenegro.com**

Visit Montenegro Digital Edition

Visit-Montenegro.com, leading web portal for Montenegro, start with publishing some of great and very useful digital and printed books, guides and magazines.

You can find many information about Montenegro and all main tourist destination in Montenegro. Wide range of interesting articles and information, but also many great and unique photos, maps and links. Each digital or printed edition is great companion for every tourist who want to visit and have great holiday in Montenegro.

Wish you to enjoy in Visit Montenegro edition and to make better impression about all aspects of Montenegro. All your comments and suggestions are welcome.

Montenegro - Breathtaking Beauty

My Notes About Budva

all about BUDVA

all about BUDVA

Stari Grad
Budva

CPSIA information can be obtained
at www.ICGtesting.com
Printed in the USA
LVIC04n2240140814
399265LV00002B/4